To: Lee

May this book serve as a guide
to never give up on your dreams

"Remember the easy road often becomes
hard, and the hard road often becomes
easy"

BY

CONVERSATIONS ON CONCEPT,
INNOVATION, CRAFTSMANSHIP AND INFLUENCE

DESIGN

GLENN M. WIGGINS
CREATOR OF THE FALSE IMAGE FASHION PODCAST

CO

NT

Dedication 2

Foreword 5

Introduction 9

Chapter 1: Concept 11

Chapter 2: Innovation 41

Chapter 3: Craftsmanship 79

Chapter 3: Influence 113

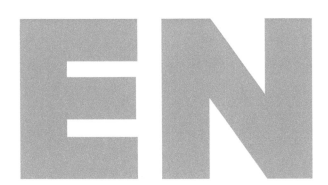

Business Contact Info   135

Glossary   136

About the Author   139

Acknowledgements   141

"

IF NOT YOU THEN WHO, IF NOT NOW THEN WHEN, YOU CAN MAKE A DIFFERENCE.

This book is dedicated to Berry Scott-King, David Scott, Patricia Wiggins, Livingston Carey, and Lee Gunn may you be proud of this body of work and rest peacefully. Also, I have to dedicate this book to my mother Mari Scott-Emanuel for being the best mother a son could ask for but for always encouraging that with keeping God first and hard work anything is possible in life . To every individual who desires to be a positive influence for their community a quote to be live by my mentor and fellow entrepreneur Darian William

FOREWORD

DR. COURTNEY A. HAMMONDS

Atlanta, Georgia

University Lecturer, Fashion Influencer, and Author

c_a_hammonds

By Design, written by Mr. Glenn Wiggins is a passionate celebration of many creative elements, especially those which are of natural origin to his professional posture, intricate structure and of fashion and style relevance. It is also a unique tribute to the many influencers who were involved in the development of this milestone project.

I was given the task of identifying how I use *concept, innovation craftsmanship and influence* throughout my career path and how others can do the same.

The ability to influence is one of the essential skills for leaders at all levels. It's more art than science, and it can be tough to get your arms around. But the bottom line is that influence matters. And as we continue to morph into an interconnected, interdependent, increasingly global workplace, it will matter more. In traditional hierarchical organizations, power is typically based on position. The higher you are on the organization or entrepreneurial chart; the more power you wield. There are clear, top-down rules where the person at the top calls the shots. *The person with the power has the influence.*

With the expansion of the industrial age and the subsequent emergence of the knowledge economy, the crafts got marginalized in the economy. Traditional crafts were just that, traditional, therefore history and only interesting as part of (cultural) heritage. In the creative arts, conceptual innovation had overtaken craftsmanship as the core competence. All this is about to change! The creative economy increasingly calls for skills that are characteristic for craftsmanship. This shows in a trend in consumer culture that stresses authenticity and quality. Craftsmanship is to meet such preferences. Craftsmanship furthermore satisfies the need for meaningful work. Mastery provides a sense of self-worth. In my opinion A strong and vital creative crafts culture has the following characteristics:

- Young people view the creative crafts as a career worth striving for
- Strong traditions of apprenticeship—A strong sense of tradition
- Recognition of the masters; fair and effective
- A strong sense of collegiality among creative craftspeople
- A spirit of creativity and innovativeness
- A strong appreciation of entrepreneurship
- A clear sense of mission (promoting and sustaining quality, contributing to a joyful and inspiring life)
- Core values clearly expressed in daily practice of craftspeople (commitment to skill and quality, innovation, collegiality and so on)

Although the emphasis of this book is on the creative arts, it contains much that will be of interest to those outside. The challenges and advancements centered around innovation, conceptualization, craftsmanship and influence within the fashion industry are beyond the scope of one dimensional philosophies. People are working on all reference points with enthusiasm, tenacity, and dedication to develop new methods of analysis and provide new solutions to keep up with the ever-changing trends. In this new age of global interconnectivity and interdependence, it is necessary to provide creative practitioners, both professionals and students, with state-of-the art knowledge on the frontiers in fashion innovation. This book is a noble step in that direction.

—DR. COURTNEY A. HAMMONDS

ERIC ADLER BORNHOP

Nashville, Tennessee

Master Tailor and Founder of Eric Adler Clothing

ericadlerclothing

The four pillars of design discussed in this book, (Concept, Innovation, Craftsmanship and Influence,) are like the systems of an organic living, breathing human body. Each is mutually reliant on the others. When they are all healthy and functioning properly, a synergy is achieved that elevates its' state of being. Similarly, when each of these four design pillars is functioning in harmony, fashion endeavors are successful.

Concept is comparable to the body's DNA at a cellular level: The concept of a product, brand, etc. forms the makeup of the organization—how it will look, smell, feel. Proceeding with the anthropomorphic metaphor, as cells grow and develop from its' DNA, the brain and body are formed. The brain is the problem-solving center of the human body. Much like our brains, innovation functions to create solutions to problems. Innovation serves the industry and my brand by providing new ways to create fashions that have never been imagined. For example,technology like 3D body scanners can capture measurements in seconds that take a human tailor 10-20 minutes to record. From the answers to solutions, our brain guides our movements just like innovation guides craftsmanship. Craftsmanship represents the body. Without a strong body, an organism is fragile and insecure. Without impressive craftsmanship a brand loses integrity and prestige. As a master tailor, I fully understand the importance of excellent construction. Craftsmanship cultivates repeat clients and drives creation forward. The fourth pillar to design, influence, is the vocal element, or mouth of the body. Just as the brain commands the language center, innovation drives influence. It creates the elements or tools used to create a narrative. Influence is how you use those tools to tell the story of your product or brand and connect with an audience. A deeply developed story and a robust storyteller can captivate an audience for an eternity.

As time passes, our bodies grow, mature and age. In the same way, the fashion industry progresses and changes through the times and trends. The inception of a concept inspires change. Change is certain, and as we innovate in the fashion industry, so do our techniques in craftsmanship. Our ability to influence our audience decides the longevity of our concepts. I invite you to maintain a healthybody and a healthy balance of concept, innovation, craftsmanship and influence in order to enjoy a long life and successful career in fashion.

—ERIC ADLER BORNHOP

ABOUT FALSE IMAGE FASHION PODCAST

False Image Fashion Podcast was an idea birthed from several years of experience within the fashion industry by Glenn Mckeva Wiggins. He felt that the fashion industry did not believe in, nor encourage, genuine human interaction. There was a surplus of interviews out within the digital realm such as with some of fashion's favorite icons, but these interviews were missing substance and vulnerability. Additionally, seldomly new information was provided during these interviews, with the exception of what you may have read in a book already. The objective of the False Image Fashion Podcast is to create a platform for individuals involved in the fashion industry to be comfortable and have a space in which they can speak from their heart. This approach encourages a story that is relatable to not only a fashion professional or enthusiast, but to the average person as well. We like to describe out work as creating a "Time Capsule" of interviews and conversations. The name "False Image" which often associated with one portraying to being something or someone he or she is not. We are changing the narrative and activating a more positive perspective one that lends itself to the very idea of true elevation and exercising the right to full freedom of expression. Instead of choosing to conform to the conventional way a fashion podcast is presented, we would revolutionize this medium.

By Design was curated to give a direct response to, or inspiration for, one's own aspirations, while also providing a storyline about individuals who use craftsmanship, concept, influence, and innovation to create a better future. This goal is not only to improve the future of the fashion industry, but for the future of the individuals as well. The conversations presented in this book are with influencers who I sought out because I found their journeys through life fascinating, and believed I could share their story with a new audience.

"

I DONT CALL THIS A STORE. WE CALL IT A CONCEPTUAL RETAIL EXPERIENCE

—HAYTHAM ELGAWLY

CONCEPT

(N.) AN ABSTRACT IDEA; A GENERAL NOTION

HAYTHAM ELGAWLY
OWNER OF THE CLEARPORT

Haytham Elgawly, ffashion designer/entrepreneur, calls himself Jersey City's "hometown hero," not shying away from being one of its tastemakers and forward-drivers of culture, be it fashion, art, or entertainment. His passion for fashion enabled him to propel numerous local brands and stores, including Eye Create and Chilltown CHILLdren, to nationwide exposure through cutting-edge designs, user-friendly structures, and unique content curation. He went on to style Puff Daddy, Rashad Jennings, Jadakiss and other celebrities. He reached his peak with The Clearport, an airport-themed fashion outlet. It greets "passengers" with "Arrival/Departure" screens that list brands the store currently carries. At its three terminals (M for men, K for kids, W for women), customers grab security-bin shopping carts. In the TSA body-scanner fitting rooms they not only try on the latest items from Akomplice, BBC, Profound Aesthetics, Publish and many others, but also take selfies of themselves in those styles with the built-in cameras to share on social media. The Clearport also has seating built in with USB-charging ports, and passengers can join The Mile High Club, a redeemable loyalty program.

Haytham was a creative director for Takeover and Sneaker Room, for which he designed and produced, respectively, the TKRS and Kolossal clothing lines, before taking it higher with The Clearport. This makes him a Jerseyite through and through, the way he's been really taking it to the streets—and 30,000 feet above the clouds. He converses with me about the importance of having a concept, and how he courageously executed his own concept into his own retail store.

© Caio Ferreira

© Caio Ferreira

Photos © Caio Ferreira

How did you go about discovering the concept behind "The Clearport"?

The idea behind The Clearport as a concept really surfaces from slang that we use every day. This slang word has been around since before we were around. When I started doing my research I said, "wow I'm late to the party, I'm just thinking about it differently". And that word is FLY. In slang terms, 'fly' means 'sharp', 'on point'—you're on another level. You know what I mean. And I used to work for several retail stores in

© Caio Ferreira

the past and I used to always pitch it to my friends like "Come get fly" and "I'm gon' get you fly. Come hit the runway". The runway started from a fashion runway. Of course, my sense and love for aviation became an actual runway and then I always called myself young Boeing 747 because I was the flyest around – that kind of thing triggered one idea. Another idea to a third idea. And then from there I said "dang, what if we built a store or a place where you got fly that looked like an airport?" and this just happened to be one of those ideas that actually makes sense.

Arrival and departure screens grace the entrance of The Clearport listing the current stockist status of your favorite brands

Grab a security bin while your shopping at The Clearport

Photos © Caio Ferreira

Did you prefer to let the concept sell itself rather the clothing sell the store?

One of the main reasons I actually went forth with this idea was because coming from that retail environment my whole life, I've seen what the do's and dont's of retail and what works and what doesn't work. The end game is to make money, so you can go ahead and try to feed your other creative ideas.

This is just the beginning. Obviously, there's other ideas that tie into this that make this a whole grand plan. And how do you do that without having the right funds for it? How do you keep this dream alive but also maintain making money? One of the answers to those questions was the concept. I don't call this a store—this isn't a retail store. We call this a conceptual retail experience. I think that's what brings clients here because in today's age and in our generation, we could go anywhere for this product. We don't have to leave our house. We can order this product online and what happens is that it's delivered to your doorstep in two to three hours through an Amazon Prime type of thing. So why are you going to get out of your comfortable warm house and come visit us? The number one reason is going to be the experience. It's going to be, "I'm going to go get fly at an airport. I'm going to go gain miles and earn this loyalty program. I'm going to go see these guys who are going to treat me like nobody else." On top of that, they also have fly products.

A lot of stores don't really invest opportunity or time into concept. I think one of the main reasons for that is go back to a lot of these conceptual ideas like this one. At The Clearport, you take up a lot of retail space for art. Art takes up a lot of space and if you can't turn around product fast enough, your brand is going to die.

How did you choose what brands would gel well with the concept?

I mean, at first I asked, "what brands do I like?". Plus, you have to remember we're really in these streets and we talk to the kids. We're in this culture and I see what people are wearing, what kids are telling me they like. So, you actually pay attention to where this culture is heading and I think you could pick or choose certain pieces at this point. Right now, it's not even about the brands anymore—it's about the pieces. The store is located in Jersey City. We're still up and coming. In that sense, the average kid gets paid $300-400 in their paycheck and they're spending $200 on Jordans. You have $200 left to spend on an outfit. A BBC hoodie costs $150 if we carried brands in that tier, which we do. But we also have to carry brands where if you want a dope hoody for $50 and to grab a pair of jeans for $60, that's $110. Look man, you still got $90 to take a girl out and still look fly.

Photos © Caio Ferreira

"

EITHER WE ARE GOING TO BE A PART OF THE CHANGE OR WE GOING TO SEE CHANGE HAPPEN.

—HAYTHAM ELGAWLY

Photos © Caio Ferreira

Were there any challenges to mapping out the interior design of the store?

At the end of the day, I'm a creative and I'm a designer. I don't care what it is—we could create furniture! Virgil Abloh, Kanye West's creative director—these dudes are breaking boundaries—that's who we watched growing up, designing certain things that were like, "What?". But then three years later we're like, "Oh, I get it". I always felt like I was ahead, and I was there but never had the right platform. That's one thing I felt like The Clearport could be: a platform and a foundation for all the creatives to grow. I mean I could never even imagine that I knew I was a decent designer. But once we started breaking it down, I started looking at the space and how we utilize it in a certain sense. I started picking up architecture books, started looking at different design websites and blogs, taking down notes and ideas and really formulating this plan of how we could utilize every single inch of this space to our liking.

But I didn't get it right. I didn't get it right all at first. There's plenty of times where there were these little kinks that nobody would notice, like, if you look at the bottom or how we had to chip off the top because there's another additional three feet up there. Don't get me wrong—we didn't get it all at first. But I'm happy with it because you know what? This is a growth process and I'm happy that everybody can be a part of it and see it grow because it gives kind of a hope for our city.

What brands or stores inspire the concept of The Clearport?

Brands that inspired me were stores like Bodega in Massachusetts, a big concept store. It looks like a grocery store when you walk in and then you walk through a vending machine and it takes you to a cherry wood chandelier hanging boutique where they sell sneakers and clothes.

I looked at Kith—how it's so clean and sleek. They call what they do 'snarkitecture'. It's really simple but it plays the same theme with the mold of sneakers and it ties into each one of their stores. They are really good at branding.

Terminal M, W, K represents the several clothing sections meaning mens, womens, and kids

Photos © Caio Ferreira

Waiting Station at The Clearport includes usb ports that allows you to charge your cellular devices

Jersey City has been considered one of America's most diverse cities—does that reflect the result of what we see here today with The Clearport?

I think that diversity affects the result of everything. I was born and raised in Jersey City. So whatever diversity this town went through and whatever it's going through now, it's all played a part in my life. My Uncle used to own a butcher shop next door, which is insane. So, now for me to have this location, have this space, and be part of the change, I think the city played a major part.

What was the actual timeline to execute an idea such as this?

I went through something really crazy last year with partnerships that I got involved with and brands that I helped build and it didn't end too well. So, I was really in a depressed state and I was like, "I've got to change my life. What do I do? Do I go back and work for a corporate office or whatever?" I took four months off and I said, "You know what? Let me design this, build this, manufacture and plug and play." So for Chinese New Year's Eve, the factories close up for a whole month. When we came back, we got it and built it out. Chinese New Year is in February and we opened The Clearport May 21st, 2016.

When the concept stops gaining financial return, what happens from there?

Is the concept gaining financial return? Because it's the product that gains that return. The concept is really just bringing people in. As long as the product is good, it's going to keep bringing in people. You just keep growing because the concept is so universal that it can never end.

Could you say there were others who serve as mentors?

One thing I've noticed about my hometown growing up is that it's always been crabs in a bucket. You can't shine because then I won't shine. Everybody placed their doubts on you or maybe that's just the people I was around at that moment. I think that's one of the main reasons I said, "When I have the opportunity to do this myself, I'm going to make myself the biggest resource and then create my own team of people that have the same mentality". That's why I have people on my team like Nvbill who shoots all my photography and does my marketing and Eric Siebs who handles my day to day operations. Eric Cease and Nvbill have their own clothing line. Bringing everything that we know together and utilizing The Clearport as a platform, as ground zero.

66

I HAD TO SELL MY CAR, SNEAKERS, DOWNGRADE MY LIVING CONDITIONS IN ORDER TO OPEN THIS STORE.

© Caio Ferreira

Full body scanner as you step out of the fitting room. The scanner takes a picture of your new outfit and allows you to share it with your friends on social media

What challenges—whether it be business or personal—come along with owning a store?

I have no anchor on me right now. I don't have no girlfriend or any kids. I live on my own. How are we going to take advantage of all this energy? People want to know what I'm doing. I'm 28 years old—I'm not making any bread. I had to sell my car and most of my sneakers just to open this store. This is real life. If you want to talk about obstacles, I moved out of my two-floor duplex and downgraded to a studio apartment. Like, I know the sacrifices I had to make in order to start something that's going to be so much bigger than me.

Photos © Caio Ferreira

Do you believe that a large part of your success in business is who you are, what you do, and how you talk to people?

It's definitely about how you speak to people and how you present yourself. Ever since grammar school, I have always been big on who I was around and what I was doing. I think the only reason I'm in the position I'm in right now is the confidence, my mind, and the most important – the gift of gab. It got me into Puffy's house in Beverly Hills. This is the type of stuff I'm talking about. I'm from Jersey City and I got into his house talking to a billionaire through the gift of gab. And it wasn't because of who I am. We are not doing anything special. Maybe we are in time but in my mind this is regular.

Photos © Caio Ferreira

© Caio Ferreira

INNOVATION

(N.) A NEW METHOD, IDEA, AND PRODUCT

SNEZHANA PADERINA
FASHION & WEARABLE TECHNOLOGY DESIGNER

Snezhana Paderina is an innovative fashion designer whose extensive background in IT and computer programming enables her to elevate modern fashion to the level of wearable technology. Her fusion of today's hi-tech with traditional fashion design has shifted her vision of style toward a combo of avant-garde and ready-to-wear clothing and bags that intersperse elements of architecture, technology, cyberpunk, literature and art throughout her silhouettes and designs. Her exclusive apparel collections include the 3D Faces Coat, the Cyborg Dress, the 3D-Printed Back Dress, a sheeny reflective fabric line featuring the Silver Jacket and Silver Pants, and Cyber Realm, a cyberpunk-inspired bag line. Her cyberpunk icon imagery extends to laptop sleeves and iPhone cases, wearable art ranging from bombers to backpacks, and polyhedron tech jewelry symbolizing the plastic geometry of 3D cyberspace.

Born and raised in Saint Petersburg, Russia, where she studied information security at the National Research University of Information Technologies, Mechanics and Optics. Snezhana is pursuing a BFA in Fashion Design from the Parsons School of Design in New York. Her designs are already making a smash in the fashion industry: Taking first place at the Fashion Futurum Accelerator by Mercedes-Benz Fashion Week in Russia, and was featured at the Metropolitan Musuem of Art Costume Institute's design competition exhibition *Manus x Machina: Fashion in an Age of Technology.*

Her cutting-edge approach to wearable technology and the process of its creation can be a mystery to consumers and fashion mavens alike. So I join Snezhana as she expounds on her fashion journey and shows us how today's fashion and tech trends depend on each other to further the growth of wearable technology.

What is innovation? How important is innovation in today's society?

I think innovation is a way to reinvent problems that we face as a society. It's an attempt to find something that needs a different approach and different view and design it all over again from the beginning. I think innovation is what moves the society forward. I find it's very interesting in my field, which is fashion and technology, that actually artists move innovation forward, even though engineers and scientists are the people that actually make it happen. Artists are the people who create the demand for innovation.

What are the misconceptions of wearable technology as it pertains to fashion?

I think wearable technology being such a young industry already has a bad reputation. I won't name the projects that contributes to this, but I think one of the biggest misconceptions is that it's something very technical or you have to be very tech savvy to use it. Usually wearable technology is geared towards the customer or the person who wants to use it.

How does technology compliment fashion?

First, it starts at the manufacturing stage. I've said before I feel there are two distinct, different directions in wearable tech. One is implementing electronics in garments, which is a very technology heavy approach. Another one is using technology to manufacture garments. For example, in my collection I use technology mostly to manufacture. I use 3-D modeling, silicone casting, and 3D printing. But when you look at my garments, you don't notice them as pieces of electronics.

© Crystal Cox

3D Render by Snezhana Paderina

Why is there a disconnection between modern technology and fashion?

I would say it's between the fashion crowd and technical people like engineers, programmers, and scientists. Both groups have very different views on what the value of a product is. I would say this is because there is a functional versus visual component. This disconnect between wearable tech and fashion happens because a visual component of wearable tech usually is not on the same level as is expected in the fashion industry. I would say the best cure is collaboration. When you look at Iris van Hepen's recent works, for example, they're beautiful usually because they are a combination of wearable art and wearable tech. That is because of collaborations between engineers and designers.

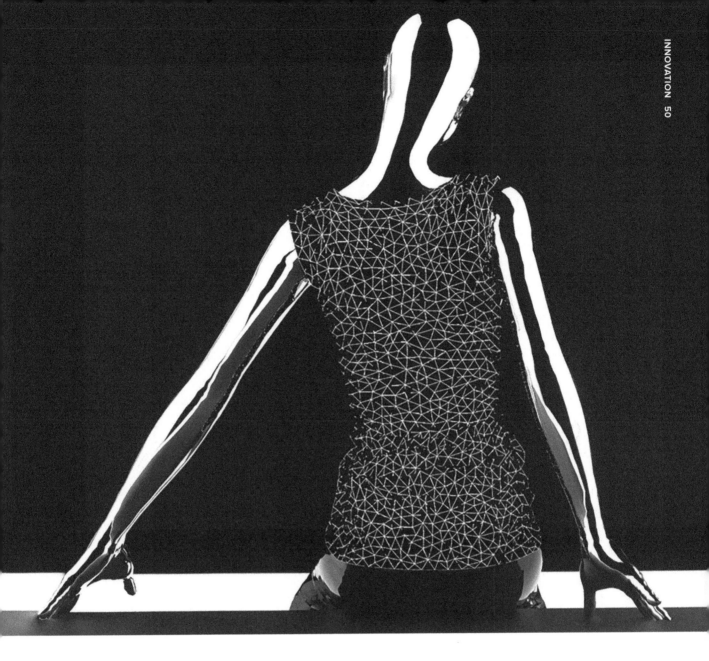

Being from St. Petersburg, Russia, did the environment itself help shape your foundation in wearable technology?

In Russia, we have amazing technical schools and engineering schools and we have a lot of programmers and physicists. I studied computer science & information security in school. I've wanted to be a programmer since I was 8 years old and at 9, I watched *The Matrix*. My degree in computer science and work experience in an information technology background gave me all the tools and the mindset I needed for becoming a fashion designer. As a designer, you use different tools in your mind.

What were some of the tools and resources you learned coming from an information technology background and applying it to fashion wearable tech?

I think it's the ability to learn technology fast. For example, programmers have to educate themselves all the time. Technology moves so fast that they have to learn new products and new software all the time. This constant learning pattern—I still use it.

What parts of cultures do you resonate with the most?

Literature affected me a lot. I love cyberpunk and Sci-Fi. People like William Gibson are a huge inspiration. Also, video games, such as *Mass Effect*.

How did the video game series, *Mass Effect* influence your designs(work)?

Character design and its characters. I collect art from *Mass Effect*—the books and all the environmental paintings—I think they're fascinating. And the characters of different races from different planets—it's a beautiful world. Starting a fashion brand is building a story and your own little world. That's what makes fashion brands unique.

How did you get introduced to the world of fashion wearable tech?

I discovered wearable technology for myself. I was a programmer, then I decided to completely change my career to fashion design. But of course, I always had some doubts. I was always into arts and towards the end of my information technology career, I just realized that as an artist, I wasn't fulfilled and I didn't feel like I wanted to dedicate my life to an information technology career. Fashion seemed the most fitting form of art for me because I love to be involved in many aspects

of my work. So in fashion, I like that I can create a product and market that product.

I always had my doubts about whether it was right to stop pursuing my career in an information technology background. Then at some point, after a few years, it just clicked that I could use all my expertise and the technology that I'm still interested in and apply it to fashion.

Photos © Crystal Cox

"
BUILDING A FASHION BRAND IS BUILDING A STORY, ITS BUILDING YOUR OWN LITTLE WORLD IS WHAT MAKES A FASHION BRAND UNIQUE.

—SNEZHANA PADERINA

Top: Glenn Wiggins & Snezhana Paderina talking innovation within her designs. Bottom: Snezhana shows us geometric shapes that is apart of her design process.

Photos © Crystal Cox

Why choose to study at Parsons School of Design?

I wanted to learn the design process. One thing about being an upcoming designer is that in the beginning, you have some idea of what garments you want to create or your perfect collection. But you have to be able to produce new collections every year. So, I wanted to learn how to use all the inspiration around me and actually channel it into designing. I created a project for applying to Parsons and it was a 3D printing project. I created a few pieces with 3D printed details, but more wearable, so you could actually wear these pieces outside of galleries. It became the first case of 3D printing in fashion in Russia, which was surprising—becoming one of the first people to apply 3D printing specifically in fashion. Three or four years ago, 3D printing and fashion just exploded, including in the United States.

How was your experience being a part of the Intel & Parsons Project?

When Parsons collaborated with Intel, it was a class with two professors from Parsons and also Intel scientists. At that time, Intel had a lab called New Devices, consisting of a lab of anthropologists, designers, and engineers, using the design process to create new devices and wearable tech. I learned a lot about teamwork. My team consisted of seven people. The biggest thing about this experience was I think it really changed my approach to wearable technologies and technology in fashion. I was always looking at it from my engineering background. For example, when you are fascinated with some technology and you really want to put it in your garment but there is no reason for it. So, I have really learned to step down and step back from my designs and really to ask myself, "Do I really need this technology in this garment or not?"

Name some of the techniques and modern technology that you use to create your designs?

Right now, I'm doing a lot of 3D modeling and 3D renders that later on I use as patterns for my fabrics or 3D printing. It's all interconnected, as in my last collection you can see I created a muse—basically a 3D model. And I used the same model, but in different forms and shapes: 3D printing and digital printing on fabric.

What is 3D printing?

So, for 3D printing, it's a technology manufacturing where machines create 3D dimensional objects layer by layer based on a digital model. And there are so many different models. Basically, it creates an object layer by layer and its fascinating because I digitally sculpt models.

What is 3D modeling?

3D modeling is the process of creating a 3D model, which is digital representation. It's like a painting but it's in 3D.

What is 3D Rendering?

It feels like photography and filmmaking because digitally, you put up lights and materials. Then you create the final illustration and final image of your model.

Top: Snezhana's first experiment with 3D printing in fashion design. The idea was to juxtapose a few different kinds of meshes and grids on top of each other, and to implement it into a garment. She chose grids that reminded her of science, math, and cyberspace. If you look closer, you can notice a hexagon tile and a Voronoi diagram. Both shoulder piece and back pieces are designed to reflect the body shape.

Bottom: Fabric Waves Shoes" for 3D printing. Its design was inspired by beautiful waves of layered thick fabric, fabric manipulations, and biomorphic fashion.Snezhana developed these shoes during a summer course "NewSkins" by Francis Bitonti in New York.

"
INNOVATION IS AN ATTEMPT TO FIND SOMETHING THAT NEEDS DIFFERENT APPROACH, DIFFERENT VIEW, AND DESIGN IT ALL OVER AGAIN FROM THE BEGINNING

—SNEZHANA PADERINA

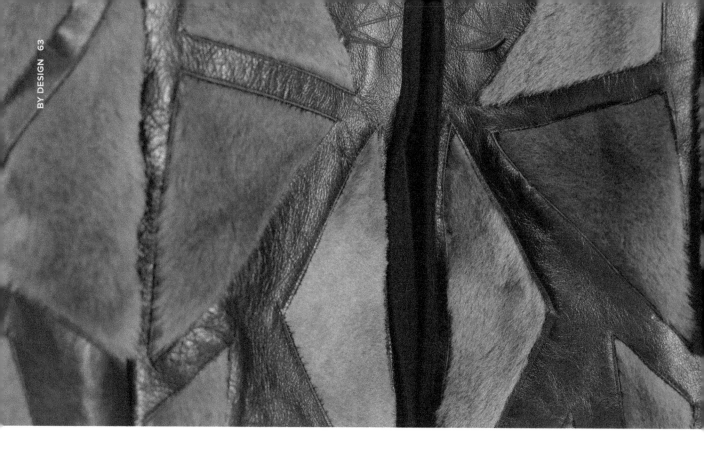

What are some things that ignite your design process?

First, I look at some outside resources as sources of inspiration. I don't follow fashion trends that much, so I'm interested mostly in architecture and literature. For me, the big part of the design process is first creating 3D renders so it's purely visual material. Then I design clothing based on my own 3D renders. I feel in that way it really becomes original.

Triangulation is fine, Intimate Decipherment, and Sea in the City are a just a few names of your collections. How did get the inspiration of the names of your collection?

Based on the content and inspiration. Taking my last collection, "Intimate Decipherment," it's the story of my muse, the virtual girl in the virtual world and the real world. It's a very personal collection. I feel it's about a person's duality. This collection started with a collection of bags, which was called Cyber Realm. The collection was about privacy and exposure to information security. What is private? I conducted group testing for the project and I realized that for every person, the concept of private is very different. For some people, the most private thing they have is their conversations with their loved ones or their photos. I did a piece after this entire project—a necklace that can store your private information with a fingerprint scanner right on the necklace. So it's not connected to your phone. So, just more secure. This intimate decipherment came from this idea of privacy and exposure.

Left: Close-up of a laser-cut leather piece from the coat that was exhibited as a finalist during the fashion competition at the Metropolitan Museum of Art by Francis Bitonti in New York. Photos © Crystal Cox

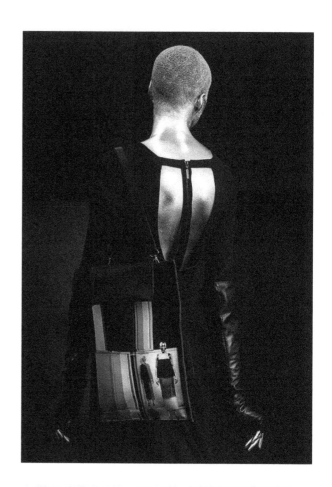

Photos © Crystal Cox

Collection Triangulation is Fine *by Snezhana Paderina was presented at the Fusion Fashion Show, New York, 2016*

"Triangulation Is Fine" is a collection that combines classic feminine silhouettes with an avant-garde approach. Snezhana used an algorithm based on the mathematical Delaunay triangulation that creates fascinating 3D shapes that she used for a fabric print. Besides an array of geo- metrical pieces, one of the looks introduces her muse, a 3D modeled platinum cyborg-girl. The collection embodies the use of technology and formal science in fashion and demonstrates how diverse fashion can be, and how technologies complement fashion.

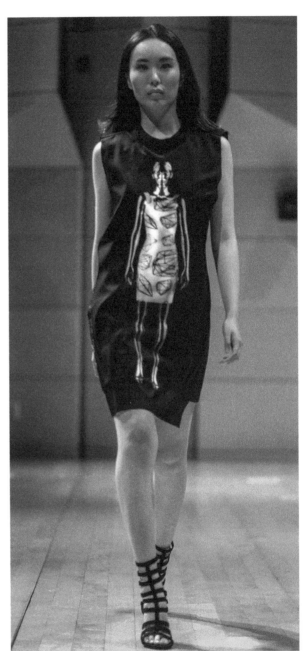

 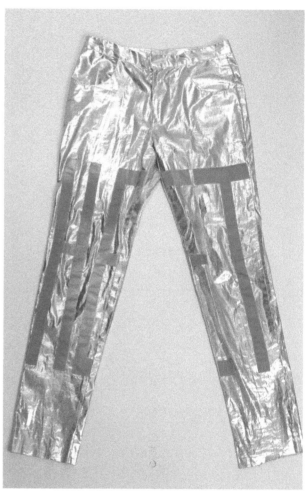

Silver pants with blue reflective fabric that says "NO" in cyrillic
Model: Joshua Mudgett

Silver jacket with pink reflective fabric that's says "CYBER" in cyrillic
Model: Brian C. Sawyer

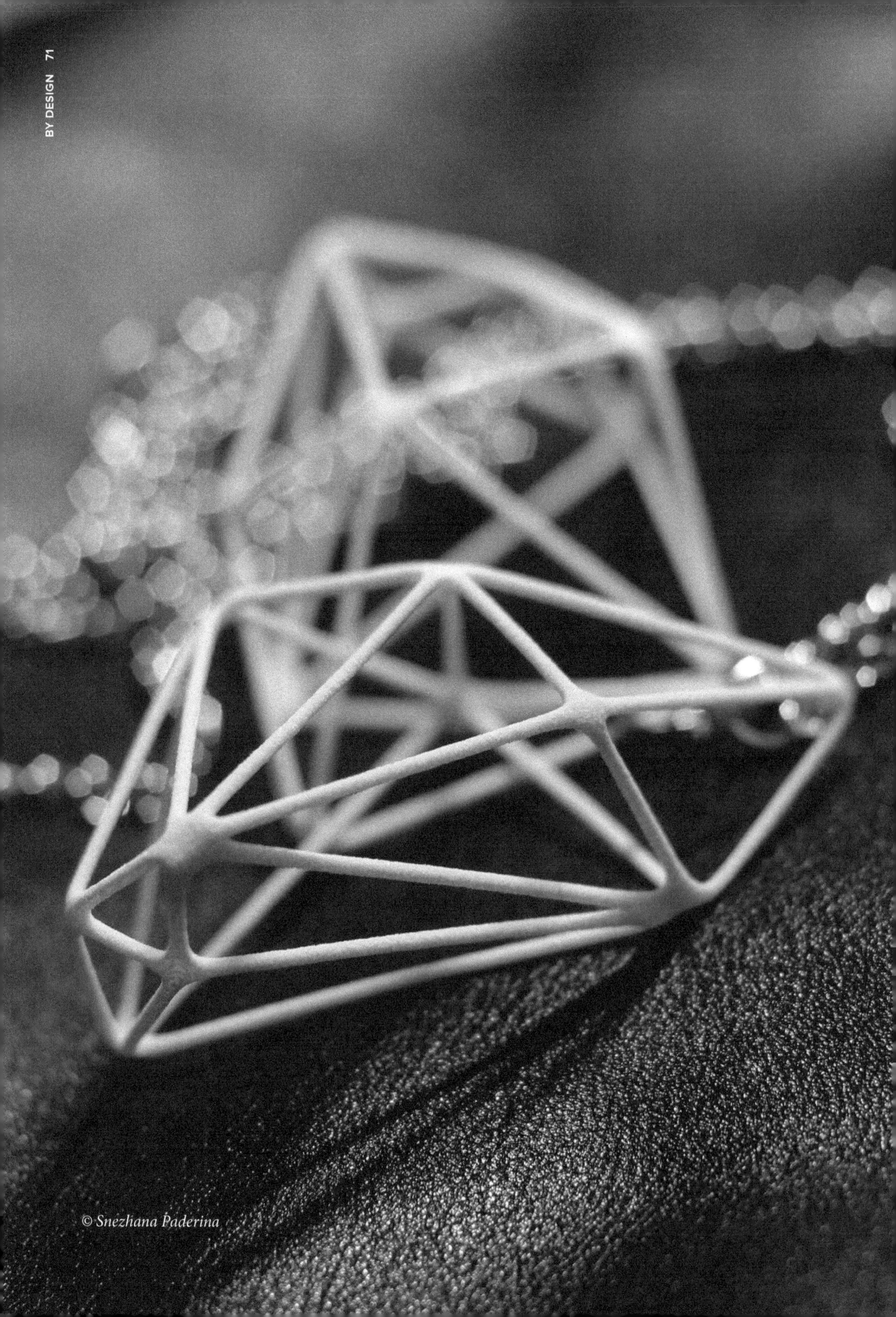

© *Snezhana Paderina*

What is the current status in the marketplace for wearable technology? Is there any infrastructure for the growth of this part of the industry?

The interest for wearable technology is definitely there and it's growing. For market opportunities, I would say for items such as the Apple Watch, for example, it is popular and successful in my opinion. Although, in fashion there is still some space and room for growing.

How can we implement more wearable tech into our daily lives?

I think technology should be more seamless and less intentional in fashion. People should notice technology like the Apple Watch is successful because everyone is already used to the concept of wearing a watch. It's still hard to grasp the concept of wearing some electronics on your body and clothes. There are so many developments in this field like *Jacquard by Google*—they are creating conductive fabrics so you don't need to wear batteries or electro boards.

What is the future of fashion?

There are so many different takes on fashion and there are so many different expectations of fashion. So, of course I want to say that technology is the future of the fashion but I also believe that couture fashion I think has its place in the future. So, I think that in the future, fashion will move away from fast fashion because fast fashion did not affect the fashion industry in a good way. I think people will be tired of it and consumers will actually appreciate made to order clothing.

Photos © Crystal Cox

How do you see yourself contributing to the future of fashion?

I try to use technology as the tools for craftsmanship. I believe there are two approaches to wearable tech and technology and fashion, which have very contradictory approaches. And I'm somewhere in the middle. The first one is engineers going into fashion because they have all the skills and technologies, but they look from the engineering tech side of it. There are fashion designers who want to try to use some new technologies as tools. Many years ago, the sewing machine was this new technology in fashion. I'm trying to use both of these approaches to push forward designs. The technology I use allows me to create designs that could never have been created before.

© Crystal Cox

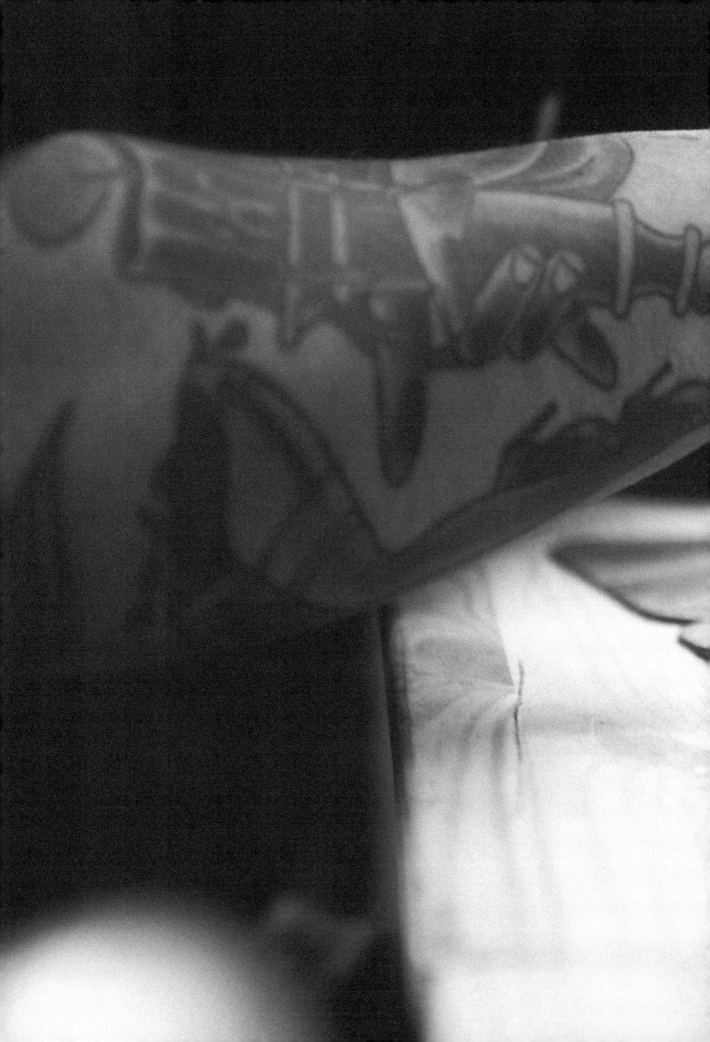

© Caio Ferreira

CRAFTSMANSHIP

(N.) THE QUALITY OF DESIGN AND WORK SHOWN
IN SOMETHING MADE BY HAND.

DANA GLAESAR
DESIGNER & FOUNDER OF SLIGHTLY ALABAMA

Dana Glaeser, founder and owner of the Slightly Alabama leather goods, bags and accessories label, had all the trappings of a successful career in corporate America, as a marketing executive for New York Life. But it didn't take long for him to realize his true calling—making handcrafted leather goods, and making them marketable and fashionable—by identifying with his roots. Memories of his grandfather making wood and leather gifts for friends and family in his red-barn workshop in Sheffield, Alabama, inspired Dana to create leather products that matter, employing the homespun craftsmanship of the needle-and-awl saddle-stitching technique handed down from generations of master craftsmen.

His products include bags, totes, portfolios, bandana rings, bifold wallets, belts, braided bracelets and lanyards, dog-collars, and other accessories. Each is cut from a single hide of premium American leather, hand-sewn right in Slightly Alabama's Ridgewood, NY studio, and branded with a lifetime guarantee. These special products trademark Slightly Alabama as a trumpeter of quality over quantity in its use of traditional techniques that celebrate the process as much as the product, like an artist painting a canvas or a vocalist rehearsing an aria before the performance. Dana dives into how his rural Alabama roots led him into leather-working and expounds on the importance of quality craftsmanship in today's digital prefab society.

© Caio Ferreira

You stated that this business started manifesting 30 years ago.

Yeah that's kind of in our description of who we are as our brand backstory—this notion that there are a lot of hallmarks in the development of any company or any brand. The day you get your business license, the day you start your website, and the day you hire your first employee—those are all hallmarks that you can say for "when we became a business". But the truth of the matter is when you start a brand and a business that is so particularly personal as Slightly Alabama, you have to look at it as being part of your entire life. For me, I talk about the fact that this business started 30 or 40 years ago and I'm not quite 40 yet so I can say that. But about 30 years ago, I was growing up in northern Alabama and visiting my grandparents and learning and falling in love with the work of hand craftsmanship and designing and making things with my hands. I headed down a path from school to college to a professional career path and then went through an evolution in many ways as a human being, to understand what it is my calling or passion in life is. It went straight back to those very beginning days of just working with my grandfather in his workshop or painting or drawing. So, that's kind of in many ways where this business came from, while our business was officially founded in October 2013. The business didn't start then—it started a long time ago.

Would you say growing up in Northern Alabama exposed you to what true craftsmanship was?

Sure, I mean, that's where I learned it from. I think in many ways more globally speaking the brand is really about roots; about where we come from. For me that's from northern Alabama but for someone else that might be somewhere in Washington or somewhere in Ohio. That's where I learned craftsmanship—from my family. That's where I explored craftsmanship just as a way to avoid boredom. Certainly, I grew up playing sports but that was not necessarily as significant a part of who I was as painting and drawing and working in a woodshop was. Those crafts felt so much more self-satisfying and on some level, very natural to me. My grandmother on my father's side was an interior designer and she had an interior design shop in Decatur, Alabama. So, I would spend a lot of time in the back warehouse of her design shop playing with all of her drafting tools that she would give me.

My grandfather had this red barn wood shop for me. As a kid, it felt like it was probably the largest the biggest wood shop in the world. But certainly, that memory of the sawdust and the smell of the sawdust and just how cool all those tools were was something that I deeply connected with.

Photos: © Caio Ferreira

© Caio Ferreira

Your mother providing your sibling and yourself with a room in your house to practice arts and crafts—what effects did that have on you?

I think probably all of the relatives in my family, from what I remember, appreciated or enjoyed crafts and my mother had a craft room in our house growing up. This room was one of the things that I guess she enjoyed sharing with my sister. She believed what was important to the cultivation of her children was not just sports and academics, but also I think that artistic side. So, during the summer we would go to the local ceramics shop and we would pick out pottery or we would paint. I don't know why she did that, but I know personally I gravitated heavily towards it. I don't know that my sister enjoyed it as much as I did. I just enjoyed the act of putting something together and making things.

Later in life, you transition those tools you developed into the need to express yourself as an individual and to discover your voice. This means using those skills to then not recreate something you saw in a craft book, but to develop your own voice, to design and make your own products, and to see the way in which that expression through your brand itself became a part of your story and your place in the world. I hate to say that what we do is art because it certainly is not art, but there is this kind of similar quality of "I have a voice, I have a vision, and I fight to see that vision come through". We rely on our craft and our skill to kind of express that. You know, we're not just doing crafts for the sake of craftsmanship, we're not just making anything, we're making stuff that particularly is an embodiment and a reflection of who I want to be in the world.

How did you find yourself going to college majoring in something completely outside of design or the arts?

It's a foolish and embarrassing story to tell partly because I actually went to Florida State University as a film major. I wanted to become a film writer and film director. I had this foolish notion that if I wanted to make great movies, I needed to study the greatest storytellers of all time. So instead of studying film, I wanted to study literature so I could study great writers. I think that may have been a cop out, to be completely fair. I had always loved books and always loved reading growing up. And I think probably more importantly, that showed how conflicted I was about what I wanted to pursue.

Obviously, I wanted to pursue something in the creative arts but I wasn't quite certain what it was going to be because I had so many passions for so many different things. I often think about the fact that in some ways, building a brand like mine is also about telling the story of what we do. And so it's probably not very dissimilar to studying literature—where you say, "storytelling"— we're telling a story through our brand in some way shape or form. This is just an example of me not quite knowing what I wanted to do with my life.

Photos © Caio Ferreira

"

WE'RE NOT JUST DOING CRAFT FOR THE SAKE OF CRAFTSMANSHIP.

—DANA GLAESAR

You became a high school teacher after college. Was this a continuation of not knowing exactly what you wanted to do?

I think part of it was that I graduated college and I just needed a job. I had applied for two jobs. One was to become an editor and the other one was to become a teacher and I got offered the teacher job first. So, I went full force for the teaching thing and I really enjoyed it. I spent six years doing that and then I think after a while, I realized I hadn't quite discovered what I wanted to do. But I was wanting to explore a lot of things. So I left that job shortly thereafter. So I don't know that I think of those things as mistakes or mis-starts; they were continuations of getting to where I am today. I used those skills, for example, at Slightly Alabama we have an apprenticeship program in our shop where we teach people leatherworking. That all comes from my experience as a teacher—building programs on how to teach this. I teach workshops on a regular basis on leatherworking, so I guess you could say those things were all necessary prerequisites to be the type of business owner I am today. I think teaching is a skill that takes time and it takes experience and if I wanted to build a true apprenticeship program, I probably needed that experience of knowing how to be a teacher and how people learn.

You went on to working in the advertising industry—an industry that has many perceptions. What did you learn from working in advertising?

Advertising is actually a world where you are supposed to use creativity. Copywriting, graphic design, web design and filmmaking are all creative expressions that are purely for a commercial purpose. I think we believe we can only have a real career, or at least I grew up in a world where I believed you could only have a real career, if you did serious things like go into business or become a doctor, accountant or a banker. In the advertising world, you can see that creatives actually thrive. For me as a business owner, I see the different legs that are necessary to build a good brand. I got to see the way in which messaging, branding, photography, and social media come together to build a good business. I also got to learn how capable I could be at doing some of those things – not necessarily excelling at them, but doing them well enough to build a brand. So when I built Slightly Alabama I wasn't afraid of how we were going to come up with the logo, how we were going to build a website or how we were going to do photography. I already knew how we were going to do all those things that were necessary and how to do them on a professional level.

I had close to 10 years of experience in doing these things both on the small advertising agency side and then later on the client side, where I worked inside the creative department of a single client. But it's a wonderful experience.

What was the out of body experience you had that got you to leave Corporate America?

It was an exploration of happiness and understanding what happiness was. I had been very successful professionally at this point, working in New York at a corporation and I had the kind of salary that you might respect for someone who has a career. I began to explore the notion of happiness for myself and what it actually meant. A very simple idea that came to me was this notion that we don't work towards happiness, we work from happiness—that if you work from happiness you can achieve great things. But if you work towards happiness, you will always change goal lines and as you change the goal line, you are actually probably not working at your full capacity.

I stepped back and said, "I'm going to try to work from happiness in my life" and that led me to ask myself, "what am I really supposed to be doing with my life?" and all of that started to lead me towards these thoughts going back to growing up in Alabama and to the things that mattered the most to me as a kid. So we took this idea of craftsmanship and my passion for the life, the thing that has never left me, and built a brand around it.

For me, it was not so much about looking at a market opportunity. It was leading back to my father's grandfather's red barn workshop. I wanted to come in every day to a workshop and I wanted every day to work from a studio, not from a silly stuffy office in a suit and tie. And then I decided let's just start – we've got to start from the very first thing, which is our brand.

My wife and I were talking and she asked me, "Why do you want to do this and what is important to you about this?" And I said, "In some way shape or form, this all goes back to my growing up in Alabama" and then it clicked and I said, "Slightly Alabama". So, I developed that name and it felt like we had crossed the first hurdle.

Then what happened is about four or five months later, maybe less than that, speaking with one of my friends one night about it, I said to him, "I believe so much in this idea that I would be happy to fail at it. So if I gave everything I had and I still failed at doing this, I would be happy with what I had done". And his response to me was, "I don't think you would be happy if you succeeded at something else". And that notion was absolutely right.

© Caio Ferreira

How did you package the name and the logo to be such a perfect match?

The logo is a little bit trickier. I was brave enough to believe I could design my own logo but smart enough to know that I shouldn't design my own logo and that I should go to a professional. This is the exciting thing about starting a brand like this. As I started to tell people, so many people joined in and said they wanted to be a part of it and a very dear friend of mine—a guy named Peter Noah who is a very talented art director and graphic designer—volunteered to help me design the logo and designed a beautiful logo. And we went through an experience of asking like, "What are some things that embody the brand? What embodies the work that you do every single day?" When he designed our logo, we took a look at the most important tool that defines who we are and what we do and we decided it's the wing divider tool. He used that, along with this notion of creating a badge, which in many ways is supposed to be reflective of a badge or a seal that embodies heritage, to design in a way that felt very fresh, very modern, and also very universal.

So, we could use the wing divider mark, the word mark, the full badge, and we could twist the wing divider however we wanted to. So, it became very functional in design. That activity was actually a very practical activity around the nature of the products. We knew that we would be branding the products themselves, and so a lot of our products have just that wing divider on there. It's also very fortunate that the wing divider logo is an 'A' for 'Alabama'. So, there was a lot of thought going into that, but I think that it's an important question to ask because when I started, I decided to pursue building this brand. I went all in and we started with the foundational pieces, which was, "What is going to be our name?" and we would not move forward until we had the right name.

Once we had that, we moved on to the next thing, which was "What's going to be our logo?" and we did not move forward until we had the right logo. We started to build slowly on the foundational things and apply our trademark to each of those elements, so that we laid a solid foundation. We wanted to build a brand that was not a hobby and never should look like a hobby—this was going to be a global, professional high end fashion brand.

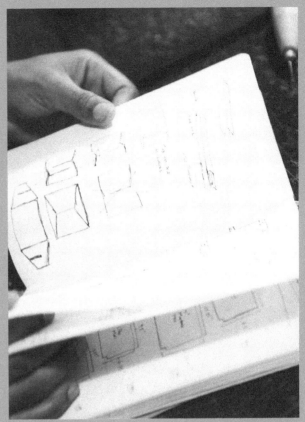

Photos © Caio Ferreira

"

UNDERSTANDING THE HISTORY AND HERITAGE OF DESIGN BUT ALSO MAKING SURE WE ARE BUILDING SOMETHING GOOD ENOUGH THAT WE DEVELOP OUR OWN VOICE

—DANA GLAESAR

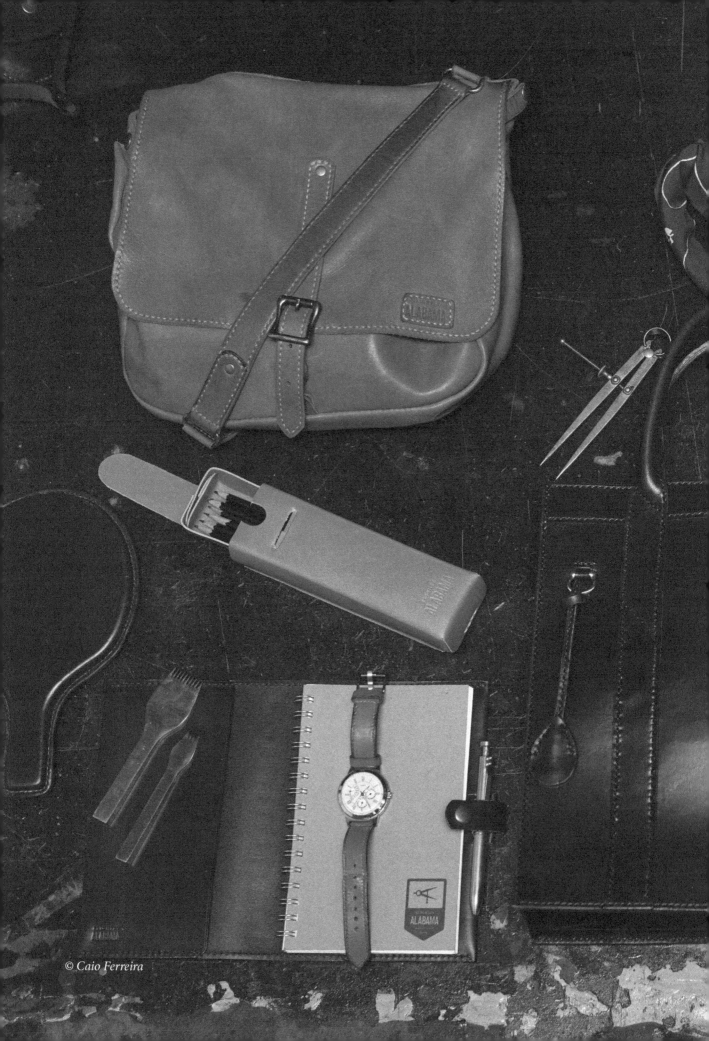

© Caio Ferreira

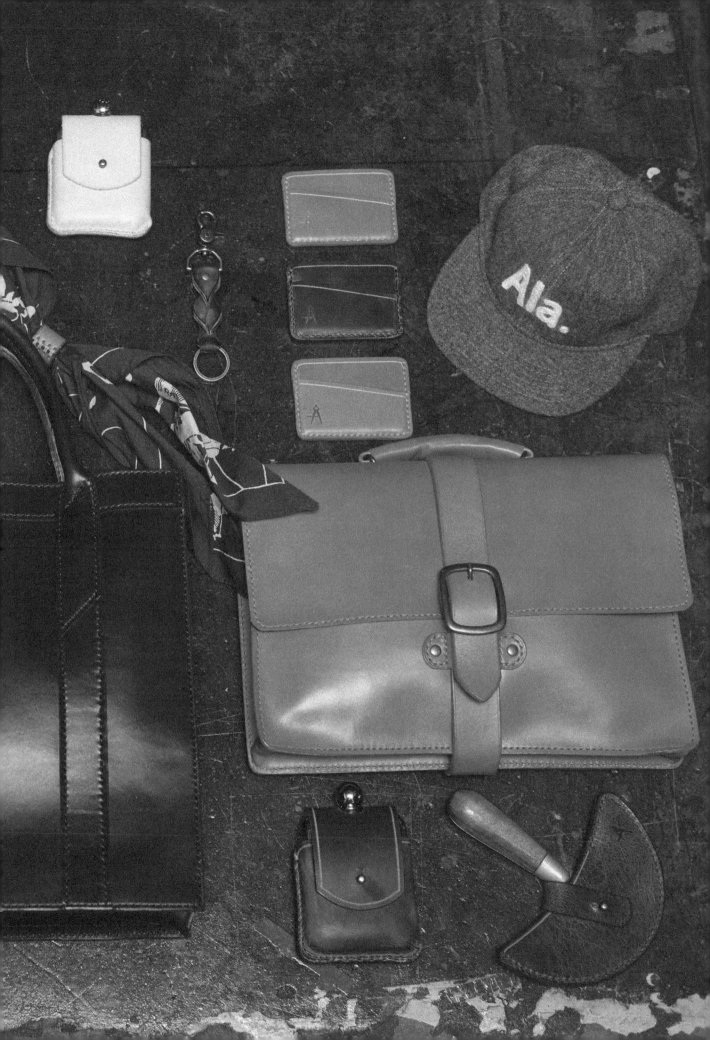

© Caio Ferreira

How did you discover the techniques in order for you to make the products of Slightly Alabama?

No one ever trained me, so I am self-taught. I'm a bit of an obsessive researcher, so I spend a lot of time understanding what else exists in the marketplace out there. I do this research so that I can make sure that those great brands or great designers are helping to establish what feels relevant in the world of fashion and accessories. So, I think it's important for me to understand and study that so that I can understand what relevancy looks like

We also need to understand a little bit of tradition and heritage behind design and what design is supposed to be. Whether we study it from architects like Eero Saarinen or from great designers like Dieter Rams and his design principles, we need to develop a philosophy of design and understand what good design is out there. But then we also need to make sure that we build something that's different enough from those things that we're developing our own voice. So, lots of research, lots of trial and error, and then there's a few things that are foundational to me as a designer that I believe are characteristics of great design, and they will always play a role in our product.

So, for me this notion of juxtaposition and symmetry and asymmetry are very important, and so is being able to play with that balance. So, we do a lot of things with S curves that are kind of asymmetrical. We do a lot of things where a particular piece, if turned a certain way is completely symmetrical but turned a different way, it's completely asymmetrical. I play with that and then also we always bring in our stitch line as kind of a hallmark of the design itself, which helps to define the craftsmanship that we are known for because we don't use a sewing machine. My stuff is never too minimalist and it's never too heavily embellished. I think our design is a proper nod towards minimalism but with just enough embellishment that it creates a little bit of visual fun or visual play on a piece.

That being said, today we're going through an exercise of rebuilding and rebooting the brand in some ways. I should say, rebooting the brand by studying it and for that, what we're doing is we're going back to the old school branding techniques of defining who the Slightly Alabama man is. By defining what he is and what he's not and what his lifestyle look likes, we can begin to build in our minds a character that we want the ideal, slightly older man to look and feel like, so that we design products for that person going forward.

Why do you choose to make your products by hand instead of machine? And what is the distinction between the two?

The most important thing to know about that is that when a leather accessory is hand-stitched, it is going to be much more durable and stronger than something that is machine sewn. So, we provide our products with a lifetime warranty, but when you have something that is hand-stitched, it is by nature and by the construction of hand stitching going to last longer than something that was machine sewn.

This is true mainly because when you machine sew something, it's two threads that are running parallel to each other that lock around each other. If one of those threads were to pop, the whole thing could unravel. When you're doing something by hand, it's a single thread that goes back and forth through the leather. If one of those threads were to pop, it wouldn't be able to unravel and would be easily repaired. When you combine that with the type of threads we use and the type of leather we use, you're going to have a piece that is much more durable. So, that's kind of our positioning on a product for Slightly Alabama – we genuinely think these are evergreen products that are always going to be relevant; today and hopefully 10 years or 20 years from now. And they are going to last for quite a long time. And not just the lifetime warranty is important but also the fact that if something goes wrong with that product, you can send it to us and we will repair it and that repair is going to be another mark of your individual product.

What are some key principles that someone needs to know when creating any type of product?

I think it's important to do the foundational work and research in order to establish what your principles of design are and what the principles of your own brand are. Always work from that exact same space. I think the work that you put into researching, writing, and thinking creatively before you even begin to design is absolutely key in making sure you always come from that space. Dieter Rams has 10 principles of good design. These are foundational principles that all good design should adhere to. So, you measure against those principles. That's what you have to do first and foremost. Having ethical principles is very important and part of that is opposing mass consumerism products that are easily thrown away or replaced. I think you have to develop that kind of design ethics before you go into designing anything and then everything will come out of that.

There's this idea that creativity should have no boundaries or no limits and I think that's a bogus idea. Not only myself but most people who are designers or writers or painters think that creativity works the best when it's inside of parameters and when it's inside of guidelines. Establish your design ethics and principles first and foremost and be able to clearly articulate what those things are and then you can be free to create something that has some sense of truth to it. And it's always going to find a customer somewhere. I think if you spend too much time trying to be timely or focusing on what seems to be really popular or trendy right now or just going after a customer before trying to understand him, you're going

Left: Brown Box Tote includes 3 interior pockets and a key lanyard (far left)
Right: River Flask. Photos © Caio Ferreira

to design without a foundation of truth and honesty. But if you start with your own timeless principles and come from that space, I think you'll always create great products and you'll evolve as a designer as opposed to becoming stagnant.

Love of the process or the finished product?

The process always. I think there is always that moment when you finish a piece and sit back and look at it, but for me it's always a slightly depressing moment even when we've achieved what I wanted to achieve. There's this moment of sadness that the process is over and immediately you start thinking about the very next piece that you want to make and it's like staring at a blank canvas, which is always frightening. But it's always the process where there's the greatest amount of satisfaction as well as the later stages of the process when you start to see things coming together and there's still work left to do.

Top: Portfolio Tan Brief with two interior pockets and one exterior pocket

Bottom: Journeyman Rucksack large interior pocket also as a sleeve to protect your laptop or tablet and the external pocket is ideal for accessories

Top: Bifold Wallet, Journal Slip, Slant Card Wallets, Fold-Over Card Wallets

Bottom: Greene Street Tote large internal compartment can carry everything for work, the gym or travel.

Carry it by hand or use the additional shoulder strap

Photos © Rand Williams

© Caio Ferreira

"

I BELIEVE SO MUCH IN THIS IDEA THAT I WOULD BE HAPPY TO FAIL AT IT

—DANA GLAESAR

66
HINDSIGHT INFORMS FORESIGHT

© Claire Petersen

INFLUENCE

(N.) A PERSON OR THING WITH THE CAPACITY OR POWER
TO HAVE AN EFFECT ON SOMEONE OR SOMETHING

MARCUS TEO
CREATIVE DIRECTOR

Marcus Teo is president and creative director of Teo Creative Inc., a fashion, luxury, design and lifestyle branding/advertising agency specializing in multi-channel communication through visual design and photography. In that role he has provided multi-tiered design, fashion consulting, image/specialty book design, video/film direction and more for the likes of Brooks Brothers, Jack Nicklaus, Penguin and LINCS by David Chu, and launched *W Jewelry* and *HOME Furnishings Now* magazines. Teo aims for the highest creative expression of a brand's distinctive characteristics, focusing on its identity establishment in the marketplace and its longterm growth aspirations, through pioneering design and photography that stands out in all media channels.

Before founding Teo Creative in 2009, Marcus was senior vice president and global creative director of Georg Jensen. In that role he positioned the famed Danish luxury brand to be a global trendsetter and culture-shaper with a multi-layered media strategy running the gamut from accessories/lifestyle branding to digital marketing. As fashion director of *W Magazine's* Men's Portfolio and an editor at *Vogue, GQ* and other Condé Nast publications, he forged creative teams with some of the strongest forces in the fashion and photography industries. Having structure within his work and willingness to adapt to change sets Marcus apart from his contemporaries. In today's society, where individuals are possessed with self-appointed titles and positions, Marcus discusses the the importance of a creative director in establishing a brand's identity and maximizing its culture-shaping potential.

© Claire Petersen

What is a creative director?

These days, with fashion being a huge industry, I think creative directors exist within design when it comes to designing. I think within a fashion house, creative directors can do a lot of the design. The creative director can handle the brand component, which is basically what the image of the brand is. A creative director can also be on the business side of things where the chief creative officer overlooks marketing as well as branding. Sometimes they do not intersect and sometimes they do. I think that it really depends on the experience the creative director has. When Heidi Slimane took over Yves Saint Laurent he was quite clear on what he wanted his touch points to be. And you can see that very clearly in how the image of the brand image design completely transformed.

What about your youth lead you into becoming a creative director?

I think how I got to be a creative director was a long process and a long lifetime of gaining experience. It's just how as a child I was always influenced by photography and by film. Growing up in Malaysia where your weather is always a constant tropical weather, it's interesting that I always wanted to experience what it was like in a different climate. And by the time I started traveling it was great to experience all the different cultures, all the different people, all the different geography. But it's always the most fascinating to me to interact with different people and it's not just culture—it's how people react to their daily lives. And of course, after gaining so much insight into that as I was meeting a lot of people, somehow I wanted to go into film at an early age. So, to be honest, when I was probably about six-years-old we all went to bookstores to look at books. I asked my dad to buy me a *Vogue* magazine at that young age. Somehow, it was something I was drawn to. To be absolutely clear, film was actually a second thought. This relates back to my mom as a hairstylist—apart from running her own salon, she has also worked on many shoots. When I was much younger, she had taken me along with her to some of the shoots and because of that, I also worked on commercials. I was a child actor in commercials.

Somewhere around the age of eight or nine, I wanted to be working at a magazine. I wanted to write. I wanted to tell stories. I wanted to assign stories and work with incredible writers who have incredible points of view, so I could learn from them. I wanted to work with photographers who took these incredible pictures. I wanted to delve into the life of the stylist who styled these incredible pictures. This might be psychological – I might be saying this for the first time—but I knew somewhat as a kid that I wanted to be a magazine editor. That's what you did if you were curious about life, stories, travel; if you were curious about exploring bigger cultures than your own. I think the one thing that has always been a constant is this I followed my

© Claire Petersen

instincts. That was an instinctive response to the magazine I saw at the bookstore.

At the point of your life when you went to school for film/journalism, was this career path a secondary option to everything you had been exposed to?

Well it's not so much of an option. I became interested in film eventually only because of the possibility of writing an incredible story, which was why I was interested. I was interested in writing a narrative about different worlds, different parts of my life, and everything I've done at a young age.

After finishing your degree in film/journalism at NYU, what parts of film do you believe propelled you?

The whole process. I think, once again, when it came to magazines, I wanted to be there behind the magazine. In some ways, running the show and working on a magazine rather than just reading it helped me connect with culture. With film it's the same way – when you go into making a film you are absolutely doing a deep dive into its own bubble, its own culture, and its own story – in production as well as in the actual film.

What lead you to working for one of America's top fashion magazines, _W_ magazine?

I was fashion director of the men's portfolio. That's how I started. And I'll give you a very brief trajectory, if you will, from graduating at NYU in film and journalism. I wanted to act immediately after graduation and I think acting satisfies ego. It also satisfies the psychological pursuit that I always wanted to write and direct. In that first year of acting, it's basically banging down doors doing auditions after audition and getting rejected. I also have the advantage of being a writer, so I actually did freelance writing for a couple of magazines in Italy and Asia that paid the bills. It was kind of a very long stretch of, like, not having a sustainable life basically. So I had to get a job. Luckily, when I was growing up, I grew up between Singapore and London. I worked for Joseph on Sloane Street in retail but that was also my start of getting deeper into fashion because Joseph was such a visionary. I went on to becoming PR Director at Charivari, which was a fantastic time because just three months into my job as a PR director, Charivari was imploding—their business expanded too quickly. I needed a job and a good friend of mine at _Women's Wear Daily_ suggested that I take the job at _Daily News Record._ So, I became an editor at _The Daily News Record,_ which was the men's wear daily to women's wear daily. I wrote and I worked with photographers

THE STYLE ISSUE

M A N

CKS: NICK WOOSTER / B. AKERLUND
LAGHER / GEORGE SAMFORD

Bla

Rachel Weisz   Kara Walker
Antony Hegarty   Art Brut   Clive

NOV

WOMEN
AND HEART
DISEASE
THE WARNING
SIGNS YOU
SHOULDN'T
IGNORE

"Lips like sugar"

IA'S DEFINITIVE MEN'S JOURNAL

UGUST

about men's fashion. Nine months into that, the fashion director—Robert Bryan of *W* magazine's men's portfolio—went on to *T* magazine, the fashion supplement of the *New York Times*. Patrick McCarthy, who was the editorial director of *W* magazine and *Women's Wear Daily*, gave me the job as men's fashion director of *W* magazine.

What were some of your responsibilities as the men's fashion director at *W* magazine?

For one, I had to cover every single brand that was out there, of which there were as many as there are now. I created relationships with them. We also reviewed the fashion shows. We covered all the fashions, but the most important thing was to do the fashion shoots, which was basically to come up with the best photographers, come up with the story and the concept, go out and do a shoot, and come back with the best images ever. At *W* magazine, I had to balance an equal amount of fashion shoots and still life shoots, which actually brings me to that introvert & extrovert characteristic. In a fashion shoot, it's an extrovert environment. It's an extroverted, organized activity: the fashion shoot, the locations, the models, and getting the actual image but also dealing with so many different sociological and psychological personalities and egos. All that goes into a fashion shoot. In still life, it's you and the object or the objects in front of you. You have utter control there but you're also in this little, tiny micro-bubble. It was a period where *W* magazine was just changing from its broadsheet format to a full-fledged magazine. So, it was a time where Dennis

Freedman was a creative director who was culminating relationships with the best photographers in the world. People were not quite sure because *W* magazine at the beginning was not *W* magazine today. It was Dennis who brought in Bruce Weber and all best photographers to work with. Luckily at that time too, I was a young stylist & fashion director, so we were all growing together. My film experience had given me an end in wanting to create images and that's where I came from in terms of concepts and story. I think I always wanted my fashion shoot to have a rich narrative to it. So, I like to use fashion as one of the tools for telling a great story.

What moment did you realize you had established your own voice?

I would say—and this is not from an egotistical point of view—I think the voice and the point of view has always been there. I was searching for the right medium as a child.

Would you say you had the right opportunity or moment?

The best life that you can ever get is the one where you're able to do what you love, obviously. I'll knock on wood for this one because I've always been able to do what I love. The magazine world was not always perfect because it is a business. I think I have focused a lot on creating images and stories instead of minding the business aspect.

© Claire Petersen

" THE IDEA OF STRUCTURE IS WHAT SEPARATES A CREATIVE DIRECTOR AND SOMEONE ELSE WHO IS JUST CREATIVE

—MARCUS TEO

How did you find yourself becoming a freelancer?

After *W* magazine had a change of guard. The entire old guard—Patrick McCarthy who was our editorial director left and Stefano Tonchie became editor in chief at *W* magazine. Having worked on a freelance level with companies like Brooks Brothers doing creative direction and branding, I kind of wanted to delve into that. I became more interested in the business of fashion and also in bringing to clients the experience of a full creative background. So I went and started doing creative direction out of somewhat necessity but also because it was kind of what I wanted to do. It was also the start of when you could tell stories online and the start of new media more in the digital space.

How did you find clients or what were the first steps in building a business as a creative director?

Relationships I already had with a lot of the fashion brands from being an editor knew that I was around. So, through connections and through people I've already known, I've been referred to different brands. So, when I became a creative director, it was pounding the pavement basically—calling, talking, and meeting people—really trying to convince them that I can really create the image for them and tell their story.

Whether it be relationships, knowledge, or location, which one is essential to a creative director?

You have to know what to do. That voice that you were talking about and that point of view that is a constant, that's what I've always had. I remember that I'm searching for the medium; searching for the right client. Second to having that point of view is having relationships because they allow me to be able to talk to others from a more direct point of view. When I say relationships I mean having to know more people and having to know the brands and the people involved in them. When I say brand I'm talking a lot about a fashion label. Brands are very important to the owners and the designers who started them. When you walk in as a creative director and tell these owners that you are the one to tell the brand's story, how do you connect with them? You do have to have an instinct and a certain affinity for it.

Being appointed creative director of the Danish luxury brand Georg Jensen, what was the bigger picture you had in mind for the brand?

The big picture is to tell the story and to harness new media. It goes right back to the past—to tell the Georg Jensen story to an existing audience and a brand new consumer group. When I got the call from the CEO David Chu offering me the job, it was the most natural thing for people who knew me. People knew I had such a deep love for design and they understood I was also very aware of the different product categories of Georg Jensen. When I went into the meeting with the Georg Jensen team, the big conversation was: we are a jewelry house, we are a home and interior house, we are a house that produces all these incredible silver from the past, we produce watches, we have men's

© Claire Petersen

accessories. They were having a little bit of a focus issue and they were asking, "how do we tell this brand story?" And funnily enough to me, it was the most natural answer: "You are a design house". It's always worked in collaborative design since the day Georg Jensen started. So I think that kind of sealed the job, if you will, because of that clear understanding and that story I wanted to tell was: Georg Jensen is the house of design.

How is the success of a creative director measured?

The story that you are telling and the message that you are creating reaches the audience. You connect with the audience, which for a brand is pretty much a consumer.

That would be a success on the business side because you're convincing people of the image or the brand or the history of the story behind the brand. Ultimately, that translates to brand loyalty. Of course, the profit and loss reflects that somehow. You want people to buy the products, which is why I think a company that deals with design across the board should really take care of the product that they produce. I'm very conscious that design needs to be completely linked with marketing.

You know sometimes in some companies those two things (design and marketing) are treated so separately. The success of Georg Jensen was having a creative director oversee the different components that make up the big picture in the different departments.

© *Claire Petersen*

These components need to speak the same story. So, whether it's the business, the marketing or design, we need to tell one consistent story.

How does a creative director educate him or herself?

Learn everything. Be curious. These days, fashion has become a second nature to me. We know how to get our fashion information. But everything that affects creative direction work really relies on the timeliness of what you do. I think a brand can be a heritage brand but a brand also needs to be vital. It also needs to be relevant and current. So when I say you need to be curious and learn everything, I do mean you need to be caught up on current affairs. You need to be caught up on technology. You need to be caught up on scientific achievements, because ultimately it's what people are affected by. To be able to convey a message you need to know what people are interested in.

What advice would help those who have thoughts on, or even are currently creative directors?

I think it's just constantly learning about things and that will ultimately inform what you do on a creative level.

"

THE BEST LIFE YOU COULD EVER GET IS THE ONE WHERE YOU ABLE TO DO WHAT YOU LOVE

—MARCUS TEO

THE CLEARPORT

759A Bergen Avenue Jersey City, NJ 07306
Store Hours: M-W 11-7pm, Thu-Sat 11-8pm, Sun:,Closed
201-706-3225 🔲theclrprt 🅵The Clearport 🐦theclrpt

SNEZHANA PADERINA

🔲snezhananyc 🅵Snezhana.NYC
www.snezhana.nyc

SLIGHTLY ALABAMA

🔲slightlyalabama 🅵Slightly Alabama 🐦slightlyalabama
www.slightlyalabama.com

MARCUS TEO

🔲marcusteonyc 🐦marcusteonyc
www.marcusteo.com

GLOSSARY

3D printing: A process of making three dimensional solid objects from a digital file.

3D modeling: A process of creating a 3D representation of any surface or object by manipulating polygons, edges, and vertices in simulated 3D space.

3D rendering: A creative process that is similar to photography or cinematography, because you are lighting and staging scenes and producing images.

Amazon Prime: Membership program apart of Amazon where you receive free two-day shipping.

Brooks Brothers: The oldest men's clothier in the United States.

Bruce Weber: American photographer most well known for his erotic and risqué work for Calvin Klein's campaigns in the 1990s.

Charivari: A fashion boutique located in NYC that was very popular and grew into a retail mini-empire during the 1970s and 1980s founded by Selma Weisner.

Daily News Record: An American newspaper which focused on the men's clothing business.

David Chu: Best known as the founder of Nautica, a men's designer outerwear company. He currently serves as the Chairman & Creative Director of Georg Jensen.

Decatur, Alabama: Known as "The River City," a city located in Northern Alabama.

Dennis Freedman: The founding creative director of _W_ magazine, where he worked for nearly two decades, before becoming the creative director of upmarket department store Barneys New York.

Dieter Rams: An industrial designer and created the ten principles of good design known as "ten commandments".

Eero Saarinen: A 20th-century Finnish American architect and industrial designer noted for his neo-futuristic style.

Florida State University: Public research university based in Tallahassee, Florida. Notable graduates are Lee Corso, Deion Sanders, Warrick Dunn, and many more.

Georg Jensen: Danish design house renowned for artistic boldness, superior craftsmanship, and creative collaborations.

Hedi Slimane: French photographer and fashion designer formerly served as the creative director for Yves Saint Laurent & Dior Homme.

Iris Van Herpen: Dutch fashion designer often hailed as a pioneer in utilizing 3D printing as a garment construction technique and as an innovator who is comfortable with using technology as one of the guiding principles in her work because of its sculptural nature and unfamiliar form.

Joseph: A fashion brand and retail chain that was established in London by Joseph Ettedgui.

Kith: A lifestyle brand and retail store that has three locations (Brooklyn, Manhattan, and Miami) founded by footwear and clothing designer Ronnie Fieg.

Mass Effect: A science fiction action role-playing third-person shooter video game series developed by the Canadian company BioWare.

New York Times: American daily newspaper founded in 1851.Considered to have the second largest circulation in the United States and is published in New York City.

New York University: A private nonprofit research university based in New York City. Notable graduates are Spike Lee, Adam Sandler, Whoopi Goldberg, Angelina Jolie, and many more.

Patrick McCarthy: The former chairman and editorial director of *W* magazine and *Women's Wear Daily*.

Robert Bryan: Former men's fashion director for *New York Times Magazine*.

Sloane Street: A major street and premier shopping avenue for the world's most revered luxury brands in London, England.

Stefano Tonchi: Currently serves as the editor of *W* magazine.

T magazine: A magazine dedicated to fashion, living, beauty, holiday, travel and design coverage which is published by *The New York Times*.

Ten Principles of Good Design:
1. Good design is innovative
2. Good design makes a product useful
3. Good design is aesthetic
4. Good design makes a product understandable
5. Good design is unobtrusive
6. Good design is honest
7. Good design is long-lasting
8. Good design is thorough down to the last detail
9. Good design is environmentally-friendly
10. Good design is as little design as possible

Virgil Abloh: American designer, DJ and stylist came to prominence as Kanye West's creative director.

Wearable Technology: Smart electronic devices that can be worn on the body as implant or accessories.

William Gibson: American fiction writer who is credited for pioneering the science fiction subgenre known as cyberpunk.

Women's Wear Daily: A fashion trade journal noted as the "Fashion bible". *WWD* delivers information and intelligence on changing trends and breaking news in the men and women's fashion, beauty and retail industries.

Yves Saint Laurent: A French luxury fashion house founded by Yves Saint Laurent and his partner, Pierre Bergé.

© Rand Williams

GLENN MCKEVA WIGGINS, JR. is a fashion entrepreneur and founder of the False Image Fashion Podcast. A native of the Toulminville neighborhood of Mobile, Alabama, Glenn grew up in an environment in which fashion was not celebrated. Yet soon after taking a few computer science courses in pursuit of a videogame design career, he needed an avenue he could truly relate to. Considering the way his mother expected him to always dress neatly with no overly baggy clothes, shirt tucked in and shoes shined before leaving the house, he realized how unique his style was compared to those of his peers, who tended to dress like each other. He always wanted to press the boundaries of apparel by wearing different pastel and bright-colored shirts and trousers. This was his way of becoming a fashion peacock among his peers, who often met it with disdain, seeing his love for fashion as just a fad instead of a form of self-expression. Even today, Glenn describes his style as "timeless, versatile, and polished."

Glenn received his B.A. in International Business & Fashion Design from Alabama A&M University, and was its first male graduate to receive the highest student award for fashion design, "Best Overall Designer." After serving as Fashion Show Director and Creative Director for the Alabama Fashion Alliance/Fashion Week Alabama, he moved to one of the world's fashion capitals, New York City, to connect with some of the most brilliant creatives and become one of the fashion industry's biggest influencers. His passion for fashion and entrepreneurship has taken him to other world-class cities such as London, Toronto and Miami, in his quest to debunk the myth that fashion is all about vanity, doesn't encourage genuine human interaction, and is only for those who can afford luxurious lifestyles.

Glenn wishes to change that narrative by highlighting the authenticity in an individual's work, coordinating industry talks to discuss fashion issues and solutions, and helping youth to build their self-confidence by encouraging them to use the power of clothing to define their individual voices and express themselves fully. Glenn is already making a splash in fashion through his False Image Fashion Podcast, on which he interviews some of the industry's most influential individuals. By Design fulfills another of his fashion visions: to publish books that put fashion in the hands of the general public so people from many walks of life can benefit from it. While taking a break from conceiving the next best idea to invoke change upon the fashion industry, Glenn enjoys mentoring and inspiring the next generation of leaders.

WITH SPECIAL THANKS

There have been many wonderful people who have spent their time in reviewing and giving helpful expert advice in getting this book finished. Below are some that deserves a special mention and my appreciation.

Jordan Washington with your ideas you help elevate the *By Design* book to the next level and those 2-3 hour conversations we would have about this I appreciate you.

Najee Wilson providing your barbering services for one of the By Design photoshoots..

Julian Howell for your time and hard work you put into this project whether it be videography or photography work.

Kendrell Trayvick for taking photos for one of the *By Design* photoshoots and being one of the first models under the False Image brand.

Derrick Ramey, Jr. for making a handmade bow tie for one of the *By Design* photoshoots and I can not wait to see the impact the Dapper Dude brand will have on the fashion industry.

Stephon Kelly one of the most talented fashion stylist I know thank you for your time and support in organizing the looks for one of the *By Design* photoshoots.

Vanessa Henderson a hidden gem in the fashion industry and a positive soul thank you for being there when I need help with any productions.

Howard Gillespie for providing creative input and wardrobe for one of the *By Design* photoshoots.

Lexander Bryant for your insightful conversations and being a continuous inspiration as your creative work has inspired this project.

Ellena Lejeune Smith thank you for your guidance and always providing a positive perspective when things didn't go as I planned them.

Kelvin Milton Jones being a listening ear, consistent supporter, and providing great advice in my most depressing moments.

Hymi Wilshire one of the first people I told about this book and everyday you reminded me the power of God to take this vision to the next level.

Joseph Roberson always being super supportive of my goals and opening up doors for allowing this book to be in the library of my middle school, Dunbar Creative and Performing Arts Magnet School.

Rose Pierrot when I lost my aunt who was a second mother in 2016 God gave me you I appreciate your family and yourself for accepting me for who I am.

Jean Pierrot I can always depend on you for a good laugh and a reality check everything was much needed.

Muriel Pierrot the little sister I never wanted all jokes aside thanks for staying up with me on late nights and providing your ideas for the contents of the book.

Kenneth Carter the best tailor I know in the world thank you for always willing to give me wisdom and knowledge not just about this industry but most importantly life in general..

Alex Williams through the process you became my pastor and your positive spirit gave me hope through hard times.

Shawn Perry providing input on a random day at Juels house.

Allison Lau help me have a clearer direction in each one of these interviews by giving me a template to follow to receive the best results.

Randy and Demi Howell opened your doors of your place of business in Season 1 to allow the podcast to host its first event you guys have been supporters from Day 1.

Lavile Russell gave me a reality check and reminded me of who I am on a random night in a night club definitely wasn't expecting it but your passionate words came from a great place.

Ed Scott one of my family members who when I fell on hard times gave me advice that force me to not get into a pity party but reminded me of my potential.

Rand Williams for being one of the best photographers I have worked with and a genuine spirit. I am looking forward to us making history again we got more work to do!

Dr. Carl Cunningham for never giving up on me and whenever I come to my hometown you always pushing me to be a better version of myself.

Dr. Courtney A. Hammonds being a mentor who on a daily serves a guide to achieving success in the fashion industry and also teaching me how to use my platform to bring about change wherever I go. Of course, thank you for writing the foreword for this book.

Eric Bornhop for writing the foreword for this book and since the first day I meet you in 2014 you have always been willing to support.

Eric Coleman one of the first members of the False Image Fashion Podcast team you recording the first ever episode for the podcast in Season 1. Thank you for your time and effort put into making this bigger than I could have imagined.

Jeremy Marc Anthony II one of my dearest friend who never lets me settle for less and always believe I can do better as a person and in my creative efforts.

Marla Johnson for being a sister and friend who never lets me forget who I am and always helps me look at the bigger picture of things in life. Thank you for helping me make the most pivotal decisions that help make this book possible you never switch up. Love you my sister and friend.

Julian "Juels" Pierrot for being a brother and friend always making sure I have balance in my life whether it is with business or personal affairs. Thank for your advice in helping making the False Image brand on what it is today since 2011 your creative input and resources have allowed the platform to reach this point now. Love you my brother and friend.

Javon Harden for being a brother & friend who no matter what happens always willing to uplift my spirits and never changing who you are since we have known each since 2000.

Alicia Brown for creating the logo for the False Image Fashion Podcast, sending countless amounts of emails, and spending long nights listening to my goals and aspirations. You help save me from me giving up on this book and for all of your efforts you will forever have a special place in my heart.

Michael Wiggins for being more than just my uncle you are one of my favorite people to learn things from. You taught me how to work Photoshop and write up my contracts. Thank you for doing things you don't have to do I love you so much.

Darian "Fry" Williams for being a father, accountability partner, mentor, friend, and coach you are what I inspired to be on an everyday basis. Thank you for your time and always not afraid to keep it real with me when I never wanted to hear the honest truth. You helped me make sound business decisions and always encouraged me to never give up on my dreams the man I am today is partly because of you.

Mari Scott-Emanuel for bbeing my mother and friend. The strongest woman I know from the time growing up I saw you work three jobs at one time while raising two kids never saw you complain. So, this book is dedicated to you for instilling in me strong morals and if you want something from life with God and hard work anything is achievable.

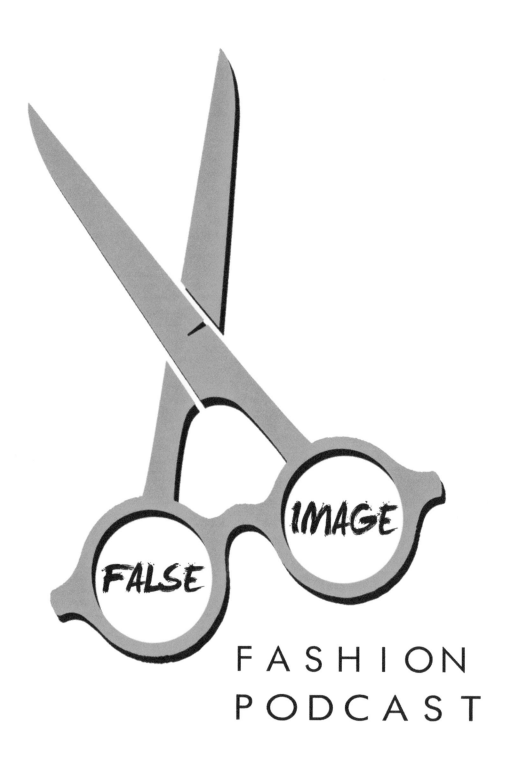

"

A DESIGN IS SOMETIMES A HEAVILY CONCENTRATED IDEA THAT EVOLVES FROM THE RESOURCES YOU HAVE AT HAND

—GLENN MCKEVA WIGGINS

ISBN: 978-0-692-12580-9 (Hardcover)

Printed by Ingram Spark., in the United States of America.

First printing edition 2018.

Glenn Mckeva Wiggins
313 Neptune Avenue
Jersey City, NJ 07305

www.glennmwiggins.com